A lizard has a slim body and a long tail.

Lizards feed on insects.

Lizards hatch from eggs, which are laid in the soil or hidden under rocks.

Lizards need the sun. This is a common lizard sitting in the sun.

In the tropics, lizards live in the houses and catch bugs and insects.

house

Shinning skinks can run up steep rocks and tree trunks.

The ring-tailed dragon runs on its back legs and jumps, to catch insects.

The basilisk lizard runs on its back legs too.

It can run across the top of a pond or river for several steps, without sinking.

The frilled lizard has a big flap of skin around its neck.

If it is attacked, it raises its frill to look bigger.

This lizard is a thorny devil.

It lives in deserts and feeds on ants.

If a lizard is attacked, it can shed its tail. The lizard runs free, and just its tail is left.

The lizard lives on and soon...

...its tail will develop again!